# Environmental Lifestyle Guide

For Grade 11 Students

VOL.8 OF 11

Agriculture

## Jahangir Asadi

Vancouver, BC CANADA

Published by: Silosa Consulting Group Inc.
Vancouver, BC  **CANADA**
Email: Info@Silosa.ca
www.silosa.ca

Ordering Information:
Quantity sales. Special discounts are available on quantity purchases by universities, schools, corporations, associations, and others. For details, contact the "Sales Department" at the above mentioned email address.

Environmental lifestyle Guide Vol.8 for Grade.11/J.Asadi —1st ed.
ISBN: 978-1-990451-82-9

# Contents

We hope that, 10,000 years from now, future generations will be able to see flowers that provide bees with nectar and pollen and...
BEES provide flowers with the means to reproduce by spreading pollen from flower to flower,....

Jahangir Asadi

This book is dedicated to my professor, Dr.Bijan Esfandiari

# Introduction

This book is part of an eleven volume series that is meant to be a standard textbook series, for grades 9 to 12. TTAIN & ESFK & SCG improves quality of life and reduces environmental degradation by fostering new consumption patterns and sustainable lifestyles through International Cooperative Extension Service programs at houses, offices, schools and libraries all over the globe.

Climate change is real. Therefore people have the potential to make a difference now and for future generations. This book provides climate science basics, including the roles that lifestyles and populations play in the climate scenario, the significance of carbon footprints, and an overview of the current climate situation. The manual has been categorized based on humanity's needs starting first with food and ending with tourism. The manual then illustrates the difference between adaptation (taking steps to live with the changes) and mitigation (taking steps to slow the rate of change.)

Adaptation examples include food, energy, transportation, recreation. Mitigation focuses on effectively engaging with local governments, through serving on advisory boards, communicating with public officials, educational institutes, schools, universities, libraries and leading communities towards climate change actions.

One useful way to mitigate climate change is through increasing public knowledge to better understand the impact of the rate of change on plants and animals. This is crucial for preserving species; and for assessing potential insects and disease outbreaks in agriculture, natural resources and public health.

Taking personal action is a key element of this manual.

Citizens are challenged to consume 20% fewer resources, to bring world consumption levels down as much as possible. Readers are given 12 practical steps to take to make the changes. The resources section provides additional information, and readers are encouraged to contact the author for further questions.

As an accessibility action, we have provided Online international courses on climate change control as well. You can access the courses via the following link:

http://TopTenAward.org

# SILOSA Consulting Group (SCG)

Silosa Consulting Group (SCG) was established to provide outstanding consulting services of management system & educational standards to individuals, groups, companies, schools, and organizations all over the globe. SCG is publishing an "Environmental Lifestyle Guide " book series as a standard textbook related to increasing environmental awareness of students means being aware of the natural environment and making choices that benefit the earth, rather than hurt it. Vol.1 to 11 (for grades 9 to 12) providing some of the ways to practice environmental awareness include: **Recycling**, **Conserving energy and water**, **Reuse, Activism, and others**.

SCG book publishing services and distribution services are connected to over 39,000 booksellers worldwide, including Apple, Amazon, Barnes & Noble, Indigo, Google Play Books, and many more. SCG has enough experiences to help create new and effective environmental educational programmes in different countries all over the world. For more detail, visit our website : http://silosa.ca and/or send your enquirer to the following email:

**info@silosa.ca**

CHAPTER 1

# About ISO 14000 for Students

The International Organization for Standardization is an independent, non-governmental organization, the members of which are the standards organizations of the 165 member countries. It is the world's largest developer of voluntary international standards and it facilitates world trade by providing common standards among nations. More than twenty thousand standards have been set, covering everything from manufactured products and technology to food safety, agriculture, and healthcare.

Kids ISO 14000s
"Kids ISO 14000s" is a new environmental education program for children, based on ISO 14000s, which is international standard for environmental management. Primary aims of this program are: -
1. To teach and train children how to manage the environmental issues (such as energy saving) by themselves through the working book and guide book of this program,
2. To certify those children who showed good accomplishment in the program from highly international authority (as is the case of ISO 14000s)
3. To network those children through the international network (Kids International Network), so that the children can work on the environment, internationally.

2. System of Kids ISO 14000s Program
The system of Kids ISO 14000s Program consists of
1. Operation Headquarter (ArTech).
2. Workbook, Guidebook (originally published by ArTech, and local versions are produced by each countries).
3. Eco-Kids-Instructors for local operation and evaluation of the performance of the children.
4. International accreditation committee for accreditation of accomplishment of the children, for certification of the Eco-Kids-Instructors, as well as overall checks of this program.
5. Linkage with international organizations (such as UNU, UNESCO, etc. …) And also national organizations

More information can be obtained :

www.ISO.org

# Canada

Environmental Sustain for Future kids established in Vancouver, BC Canada in 2020. (ESFK) is an international ecolabel focused on taking care of environment for future of kids. ESFK defined as 'self-declared' environmental claims made by manufacturers and businesses based on ISO 14020 series of standards, the claimant can declare the environmental objectives and targets in relation to taking care of environment for future kids. However, this declaration will be verifiable.

Environmental Sustain for Future Kids
Vancouver, BC CANADA

Email: info@esfk.org
Web: www.esfk.org

# All about 'Eco-friendly' garden

The environment is – rightly so – on everyone's minds, and if you have a garden, you have an opportunity to contribute to protecting the natural world.

But what does a eco-friendly garden actually look like, and what features does it have? You might imagine an untamed, overgrown jungle teeming with wildflowers and insects.

Nowadays, however, even the slickest contemporary garden designs can be environmentally friendly, thanks to a combination of ethically-sourced materials and innovative technology.

Plan your eco-friendly garden today:

# Seven ways to create an eco-friendly garden:

### 1. Recycle and Reuse Materials

Using recycled materials instead is a great way to go green. The main concern is the origin, extraction, manufacture and installation of materials in structures, paths, walls and patios.

As reclamation yards, especially those in cities, can be expensive, trawl through out-of-town yards and junk shops for materials. New' materials such as paving made from recycled concrete aggregate are now widely available and Many companies now sell pots, fencing and furniture made from recycled wood and plastic.

### 2. Looking for Ecolabelled Products

Green materials sourced and made by the local community feature strongly in sustainable gardens. Choosing them helps to reduce your carbon footprint as they have few air miles attached, plus most of them use little or no cement, the production of which accounts for more than five per cent of the world's carbon emissions. (Page 36 for more detail). They also give gardens a 'sense of place' by linking them to the local surroundings, which is especially important in rural settings. Materials such as cob (clay and straw), oak, rammed earth, log walls, woven willow, chestnut paling timber and even straw bales are full of character. You will need to consider cost versus durability more keenly than usual, but the suppliers and craftsmen will be able to advise you.

## 3. Use Local Materials

Choose materials and features, such as paving and pergolas, that have been sourced or built locally, as this will help reduce a garden's carbon footprint and support nearby businesses. For timber products and decking, look for a Forest Stewardship Council (FSC) logo, (Page 32 for more detail) for wood originating from certified plantations.

## 4. Reduce Water Consumption

Water conservation is essential, so install a butt on every downpipe – you can choose weathered oak barrels or the ubiquitous green plastic tubs. If you have the space, consider an underground rain tank. Larger ones can easily collect enough water for the average garden, plus you can set them up to flush your WC.

Clever cost-cutting irrigation helps too. Don't use a sprinkler on the garden – water the roots of plants without wasting it on the leaves (automated watering systems are useful here); repair leaky pond liners; buy large pots for plants as they don't dry out as quickly; and don't mow the lawn too low in hot weather.

## 5. Use Premeable Paving

Water run-off from concrete-covered gardens in towns and cities causes localised flooding and affects wildlife significantly. To tackle this problem, legislation has been introduced to regulate the use of solid surfaces in front gardens. You must now use permeable surfacing materials.

Crunchy gravel and slate chippings are the obvious permeable alternative to solid paving, but there are lots of other materials available – from porous asphalt and block paving to grass reinforced with recycled plastic grids.

## 6. Using Eco Roof

Green roofs are becoming increasingly popular as they help increase biodiversity, provide good insulation, improve air quality and control water run-off – they're also very attractive.

There are plenty of products available using different construction techniques – you can even retrofit an existing shed and garage if they are able to take the weight.

## 7. Choose Eco-friendly Plants

Choosing the best plants is an important design tool, especially if you're looking to create an organic garden.

In an eco-friendly garden, the best plants will provide food and shelter, creating perfect habitats for beneficial wildlife. Choose lots of local berry-producing plants and trees, such as hawthorn, which might be growing nearby – birds and insects will already be used to them, so they'll visit your garden more frequently if you grow them.

# 5 supplementary ways to create an Eco-friendly garden:

### 1.Increase wildlife and biodiversity

Encouraging wildlife makes your garden far more entertaining, as well as helping with pest control – slug-eating hedgehogs and slow-worms love piles of leaves and logs. To attract birds that help with caterpillar control, erect nest boxes and put out a variety of food. Song thrushes love dried fruit, blackbirds adore rotten apples, and sunflower seeds will attract chaffinches and blue tits.

Entice bees by choosing plants with 'open faces'; bright, showy blooms that flower throughout the year. Spring flowers are important for waking bees but are often overlooked; wallflowers, aubrietia and rosemary are all good pollen and nectar sources. For summer, catmint, thyme and lavender are particularly good. Ivy in flower is great in autumn. To help solitary bees, a special bee hotel provides the perfect nesting site.

The key principle to planting is always putting them where they're happiest. Contented plants take care of themselves, but stressed ones need constant feeding and watering, so make sure you don't plant your sun-lovers in the shade, for example, or vice versa. Matching the right plant to the right place will also help keep garden maintenance time to a minimum.

## 2. Change quality of Soil

Lots of compost and/or well-rotted manure will keep your soil in what gardeners call 'good heart'. This creates a healthy soil teeming with essential micro-organisms, which in turn gives you healthy plants that don't succumb to pests and diseases. Compost soaks up water like a sponge, too – useful in free-draining sandy soils.

Dig in a large bucketful every few feet when planting, or spread liberally around plants as a mulch each spring; this also helps stop light soils from being washed away in heavy rain.

### 3.Prepare homemade compost

Recycling green waste is important, too – homemade compost costs nothing to make, and will save money on bagged compost and soil conditioner from garden centres.

What to add to your compost:
- veg peelingswood
- hedge trimmings
- grass clippings
- tea bags
- egg boxes
- egg shells
- leaves
- shredded paper
- vacuum cleaner contents

Avoid cooked food, meat, pet faeces and glossy magazines

## 4. Limit peat-based composts

Peat is dug from peat bogs, causing irreparable damage to precious natural habitats, and as it forms very slowly, simply isn't sustainable either. The problem is that it's great for growing plants as it's sterile, easy to handle, and holds onto nutrients and water like a sponge.

To cut down your use, stop using peat as a mulch or soil conditioner, and instead use **homemade compost**, rotted farmyard manure and leaf mould, which perform better and are full of nutrients. Buy peat-free or reduced-peat compost for potting – it'll say so on the bag – and you'll now find that modern peat-based composts available to gardeners include some of the alternatives, such as bark, wood fibre, coir (coconut husk) or specially formulated green waste.

## 5. **Create a natural garden**

Plant according to the garden, not the gardener,' is the ethos at the heart of the natural garden, and looking to nature will provide inspiration and a template to follow. Work with the characteristics of your garden, not against them.

For example, in damp shade, embrace woodland plants and those that grow on woodland margins. For sunny slopes, consider Mediterranean plants like rosemary, juniper, bay and sage – plants with silvery or blue-grey leaves that have naturally adapted to such conditions. Waterlogged soil? Choose wet-land plants – not only will your planting visually sit more comfortably, but also promote happy, healthy plants and suffer fewer pests and diseases.

More popular now than ever, native plants are tough, easy to grow and provide food and valuable habitats for wildlife. Ideal for a more relaxed design, they will also help to preserve our threatened plant heritage. Favourites include spiky teasels, gunmetal-coloured cotton thistle, and hardy cranesbills. Quick to colonise poor soils and sunny walls, the red, pink or white flowers of valerian, in particular, are stunning and last for ages. Leave some parts of the garden untidy; nature likes it messy, so gather piles of leaves in undisturbed corners and collect logs and branches, rather than burn them (if they're not diseased). You'll encourage thousands of insects and foraging birds. Hedgehogs also find such spots irresistible to hibernate in.

# All about 'Eco-friendly'
# Livestock Ranching

R anching is the act of running a ranch, which is essentially an extensive farm for the sole purpose of raising livestock and crops. .... Therefore, we can bring the two definitions together to define livestock ranching as the breeding of animals, for the purpose of food or clothing production. livestock farming, raising of animals for use or for pleasure. ... Ruminant (cud-chewing) animals such as cattle, sheep, and goats convert large quantities of pasture forage, harvested roughage, or by-product feeds, as well as nonprotein nitrogen such as urea, into meat, milk, and wool.

Livestock farmers are facing a number of challenges today. Demands for a lower impact on the environment, especially reducing greenhouse gas emissions, for more animal welfare and for less intensive production need to be balanced with a stable production and a good income. While there are challenges for livestock farmers, there are also many opportunities to increase the resilience and profitability of their farms.

Sustainable pasture management can offer ways to provide good feed to dairy cattle, help reduce livestock emissions, build up and store carbon in the soil, help mitigate the effects of climate change, and much more.

Digitisation and decision support tools can support farmers in better managing their livestock, for instance for more resource- and costefficiency.

## Grazing for carbon

Grasslands have enormous potential for storing carbon (C) in the soil. Carbon sequestration improves soil health, makes soils more resilient to extreme weather events, contributes to climate change mitigation and can benefit pasture quality. In sustainable livestock grazing systems, the key challenge is to find the best type of management to combine animal production with soil ecosystem services such as carbon storage, nutrient cycling and biodiversity.

## Marketing pasture while reducing emissions

Livestock production significantly contributes to ammonia and greenhouse gas emissions, specifically methane. Adopting grazing methods that let cows graze optimally can contribute directly to lowering livestock emissions.

In addition, there is a growing interest in precision livestock farming, measuring methods, and digital tools that can support farmers in lowering, monitoring or managing farm emissions.

The 'Grazing cow monitor' project has developed a collar that uses GPS tracking to monitor the location of individual cows. The tool clearly indicates how much time a cow spends indoors or outdoors. "The monitor gives farmers digital proof that their cows have spent a sufficient amount of time grazing outdoors", It can therefore help make their administrative tasks easier, but it also allows farmers to label and market their milk as pasture milk." Giving cows access to pastures provides them with fresh grass to eat and can help maintain a healthy soil ecosystem. Outdoor grazing can also help to reduce ammonia emissions from livestock.

When the cows spend less time in the stables, this lowers the chance of faeces reacting with urine and producing ammonia. Keeping track of their cows' pasture time is one of the options for farmers in Flanders and the Netherlands to prove that they are taking measures to lower ammonia emissions.

Farmers can see the results on a dashboard, which they can easily access on their computer or smartphone.

**Strategies for managing permanent pasture**

Permanent grasslands offer many benefits for biodiversity, ecosystem services such as carbon sequestration, and animal health. Sustainable management strategies can help to maximise these benefits, for instance by matching grassland production with livestock needs.

Digital measuring and decision support tools can help increase resource efficiency and optimise grass production. Differentiating grass-based products such as meat, milk and cheese, can help create higher market value for farmers. Exchanging knowledge is key for increasing profitability, productivity and sustainability for permanent pastures all over the globe..

## Robust and resilient dairy farming

Dairy farms are currently faced with economic and environmental challenges, such as volatile prices, extreme weather events, and market demands for more animal-friendly production systems. Improving grazing management can lead to happier cows that produce quality milk with a better price for the farmer. Exchanging experiences can help farmers make their own farms more robust and resilient.

# How to create Eco friendly
# Butterfly Garden

Creating a hospitable environment will entice butterflies to stay around long enough to lay eggs for a new generation. By providing the basics of shelter, water, and food—including butterfly-friendly plants—butterflies have a greater chance of thriving and reproducing. Kids love butterflies! Encourage your child's sense of connection to the natural world and invite butterflies into your landscape by planting a butterfly garden. A butterfly garden provides a colorful array of nectar-producing plants that not only attract butterflies (and often hummingbirds as well), but offers plants to feed the caterpillar stage of their life cycle. With the appropriate plantings, a butterfly garden provides opportunities to educate your children about the life cycle of a butterfly, allowing them to view each stage of growth and explore the intricate relationships of plants and animals.

Materials:
• in-ground garden space, raised bed or container garden
• trowel or shovel
• flowering plants for adult butterfly
• host plans for caterpillars

Approximate Time to Complete: 3 to 4 hours to plan, gather plants and install; multiple weeks to grow and attract butterflies

Location: Outdoor
Ages: fun for all ages
Season: spring through fall

Start with a blank slate by pulling out dead bush, removing the plants that were overgrown, and just getting down to the bare earth.

Select plants that grow well in your area. You need to include flowering plants that attract butterflies (many butterflies have favorite plants to sip from) and also leafy "host plants" that attract egg-laying butterflies and provide food for the caterpillars (also known as the larvae). It is always best to select native plants that will attract butterflies native to your area.

### Preferred Plants For Caterpillars
Note: Planting trees and taller bushes will help give your garden the sustainability it needs to feed your caterpillars and preserve the flowers for your butterflies.

### Trees
Serviceberry, River Birch, Hackberry, Kousa Dogwood, Apple, Cherry, Plum, Willow

Here are a few examples of common butterflies
and their preferred food sources:

| Butterfly | Host plant(s) for caterpillars | Nectar plants for adult butterflies |
|---|---|---|
| Monarch | Milkweed | Milkweed, asters, red clover, zinnia, cosmos, lantana, pentas, daisy |
| Eastern Black Swallowtail | Carrots, celery, dill, parsley, Queen Anne's lace, rue, Texas turpentine broom | Milkweed, phlox |
| Giant Swallowtail | Citrus, hop tree, prickly ash, rue | Lantana, orange tree |
| American Painted Lady | Daisies, everlastings, and other composites | Burdock, daisy, everlastings, mallow, yarrow, zinnia, heliotrope |
| Orange Sulphur | White clover, alfalfa, vetch, lupine | Clovers, dandelion, parsley, zinnia, other meadow flowers, members of the composite family |
| Silver-Spotted Skipper | Beans, beggar's tick, licorice, locusts, wisteria | Many garden and meadow flower |
| Variegated Fritillary | Violets, pansies, stonecrops, passionflowers | Meadow flowers, hibiscus, composite family |

Plant your garden. Add one or two large, flat rocks in the sun so butterflies a place to bask when mornings are cool. Since butterflies cannot drink from open water, provide them with a "puddle" by filling a container, such as an old birdbath, with wet sand where they can perch and drink safely.

Once the garden is planted, stand back and wait for the butterflies to stop by. With a successful butterfly garden, your kids will be able to observe the developmental process of a butterfly.

The eggs soon hatch, and the larvae appear and eat the leafy growth of the host plant, eventually developing into full-grown caterpillars. Remember, you will need to tolerate some leaf damage from your very hungry garden guests.

Later, these caterpillars affix themselves to a twig or branch and form a chrysalis, entering the pupa stage. Within about two weeks, they metamorphose into butterflies and re-emerge. Avoid all pesticides. Butterflies are insects, so it makes sense that insecticides — even those labeled organic" — can harm them.

1) For _____ _____ and decking, look for a Forest Stewardship Council logo, for wood originating from certified plantations.
A) timber products
B) wooden box
C) Plastic Bags
D) Concreate tiles
ANSWER:

2) This creates a healthy soil teeming with essential micro-organisms, which in turn gives you healthy plants that don't succumb to pests and diseases. Dig in a large bucketful every few feet when planting or spread liberally around plants as a mulch each spring; this also helps stop light soils from being washed away in heavy rain.
A) True
B) False
ANSWER:

3) Sequestration improves soil health, makes soils more resilient to extreme.
A) True
B) False
ANSWER:

4) Lots of compost and/or well-rotted manure will keep your soil in what gardeners call 'good heart'.
A) True
B) False
ANSWER:

5) A _____ _____ provides a colorful array of nectar-producing.
A) timber products
B) butterfly garden
C) Plastic Bags
D) Concreate tiles
ANSWER:

6) To cut down your use, stop using peat as a mulch or soil conditioner, and instead use homemade compost, rotted farmyard manure and leaf mould, which perform better and are full of nutrients.
A) True
B) False
ANSWER:

7) To make and will save money on bagged compost and _____ conditioner from.
A) timber
B) soil
C) special
D) great
ANSWER:

8) In an Eco-friendly Garden, the best plants will provide food and shelter, creating perfect habitats for beneficial wildlife.
A) True
B) False
ANSWER:

9) Digitization and decision support tools can support farmers in better managing their livestock, for instance for more resource- and cost efficiency
A) True
B) False
ANSWER:

10) It can therefore help make their administrative tasks easier, but it also allows farmers to label and market their milk as pasture milk." Giving cows access to pastures provides them with fresh grass to eat and can help maintain a healthy soil ecosystem.
A) True
B) False
ANSWER:


11) _____ measuring and decision support tools can help increase resource efficiency and optimize grass production.
A) timber
B) special
C) Digital
D) great
ANSWER:


12) Weather events, contributes to climate change mitigation and can benefit.
A) True
B) False
ANSWER:

13) For sunny slopes, consider Mediterranean plants like.
A) True
B) False
ANSWER:


14) Important in rural settings. Materials such as cob, oak, rammed earth, log walls, woven willow, chestnut paling timber and even.
A) True
B) False
ANSWER:

15) Piles of leaves and logs. To attract birds that help with caterpillar, erect nest boxes and put out a variety of food.
A) True
B) False
ANSWER:

16) Recycling green waste is important, too – homemade compost costs nothing to make, and will save money on bagged compost and soil conditioner from garden centers.
A) True
B) False
ANSWER:

17) What to add to your compost:
A) veg peelings wood
B) hedge trimmings
C) grass clippings
D) tea bags
E) All of them
ANSWER:

18) Peat is dug from peat bogs, causing irreparable damage to precious natural habitats, and as it forms very slowly, simply isn't sustainable either.
A) True
B) False
ANSWER:

19) Grasslands have enormous potential for storing carbon (C) in the soil. Carbon sequestration improves soil health, makes soils more resilient to extreme weather events, contributes to climate change mitigation and can benefit pasture quality.
A) True
B) False
ANSWER:

20) Improving grazing management can lead to happier cows that produce quality milk with a better price for the farmer. Exchanging experiences can help farmers make their own farms more robust and resilient.
A) True
B) False
ANSWER:

21) By providing the basics of shelter, water, and food—including butterfly-friendly plants—butterflies have a greater chance of thriving and reproducing.
A) True
B) False
ANSWER:

22) ways to create an eco-friendly garden
A) Recycle and reuse materials
B) Choose eco materials
C) Go for local materials
D) Conserve water
E) All of them
ANSWER:

## Bibliography:

Amberg, N.; Magda, R. Environmental Pollution and Sustainability or the Impact of the Environmentally Conscious Measures of International Cosmetic Companies on Purchasing Organic Cosmetics. Visegrad J. Bioecon. Sustain. Dev. 2018, 1, 23.

Asadi, J., "International Environmental Labelling, Economic Consequencies, Export Magazine, July 2001

Asadi, J. 2008. Mobile Phone as management systems tools, ISO Magazine, Vol.8, No.1

Asadi, J., Eco-Labelling Standards, National Standard Magazine, Sep. 2004.

Barbieux, D.; Padula, A.D. Paths and Challenges of New Technologies: The Case of Nanotechnology-Based Cosmetics Development in Brazil. Adm. Sci. 2018, 8, 16.

CHOI, J.P. Brand Extension as Informational Leverage. Review of Eco- nomic Studies, Vol. 65 (1998), pp. 655-669.

Corrado, M., (1989), The Greening Consumer in Britain, MORI, London

Corrado, M., (1997), Green Behaviour – Sustainable Trends, Sustainable Lives?, MORI, london, accessed via countries. Manila, Asian Development Bank 33p.

Cosmetics, Perfume, & Hygiene in Ancient Egypt. Available online: https://www.ancient.eu/article/1061/cosmetics-perfume--hygiene-in-ancient-egypt/

He Z, Xu J X 1993 Evalustion and measurement of Landscape greening benefit J.Chinese Landscape Architecture.  03  46-51

Davies, Clive. Chief, Design for the Environment Program, EPA March 24, 2009.

EIP-AGRI network at www.eip-agri.eu

The Family Butterfly Book by Rick Mikula. Storey Publishing,

Federal Trade Commission, "Sorting Out Green Advertising Claims." http://www.ftc.gov/bcp/edu/pubs/consumer/general/gen02.shtm (March 26, 2009, March 27, 2009)

MSNBC, "Do You Know What's in Your Cleaning Products?" http://today.msnbc.msn.com/id/29663739/ (March 17, 2009)

Ooyen, Carla. Research Manager with Nutrition Business Journal. Personal correspondence. March 19, 2009.

Tekin, Jenn. Marketing Manager with Packaged Facts & SBI. Personal correspondence. March 17, 2009.

University of California - Berkeley. http://berkeley.edu/news/media/releases/2006/05/22_householdchemicals.shtml (March 26, 2009)

Feenstra, R.C. "Exact Hedonic Price Indexes," Review of Economics and Statistics 77 (1995): 634-653.

Feenstra, R.C., and J.A. Levinsohn. "Estimating Markups and Market Conduct with Multidimensional Product Attributes," Review of Economic Studies (62 (1995): 19-52.

Forest Stewardship Council: "Principles and criteria for forest stewardship" Document 1.2: <http://www.fscoax.org>

Forsyth, K. 1999. Will consumers pay more for certified wood products? Journal of Forestry 97 (2) : 18-22.

Freeman, A. M III. The Measurement of Environmental and Resource Values. Theory and Methods. Washington D.C.: Resource for the Future, 1993.

Friends of the Earth, 1993. Timber certification and eco-labeling. London, FOE:

Geetha Margret Soundri, "Ecofriendly Antimicrobial Finishing of Textiles Using Natural Extract", Journal of International Academic Research For Multidisciplinary, ISSN: 2320 – 5083, 2014, Vol 2.

Graves, P., J.C. Murdoch, M.A. Thayer, and D. Waldman. "The Robustness of Hedonic Price Estimation: Urban Air Quality," Land Economics 64(1988): 220-233.

Halvorsen, R. and R. Palmquist. "The Interpretation of Dummy Variables in Semilogarithmic Equations." American Economic Review 70:474-75 (1980).

Imhoff, Dan, and Grose, Lynda, and Carra, Roberto., "Organic Cotton Exhibit," Mimeo. Simple Life and distributed the Texas Organic Cotton Marketing Cooperative, O'Donnell, Texas (1996).

Imhoff, Dan. "Growing Pains: Organic Cotton Tests the Fibre of Growers and Manufacturers Alike," reprinted on Simple Life's web page (simplelife.com), but first printed by Farmer to Farmer, December 1995.

IISO 14020, ISO 14021,ISO 14024,ISO 14025, International Organization for Standardization.

Kennedy, P.E. "Estimation with Correctly Interpreted Dummy Variables in Semilogarithmic Equations," American Economic Review 71: 801 (1981).

Kirchho®, S., (2000), Green Business and Blue Angels.

Labeling Issues, Policies and Practices Worldwide.

Lamport, L. 1998. The cast of (timber) certifiers: who are they? International J. Ecoforestry 11(4): 118-122.

Large Scale impoverishment of Amazonian forests by logging and fire. 1999.

Lathrop, K.W. and Centner, T.J. 1998. Eco-labeling and ISO 14000: An analysis of US regulatory systems and issues concerning adoption of type II standards. Environmental

Lee, J. et al. 1996. Trade related environmental measures; sizing and comparing impacts.

Lehtonen, Markku. 1997. Criteria in Environmental Labeling: A comparative Analysis on Environmental Criteria in Selected Labeling Schemes. Geneva, UNEP. 148p.

LIEBI, T. Trusting Labels: A Matter of Numbers? Working Paper Uni versity of Bern, No. 0201 (2002).

Lindstrom, T. 1999. Forest Certification: The View from Europe's NIPFs. Journal of Forestry 97(3): 25-31. London

Losey, J.E., Rayor, L.S. & Carter, M.E. 1999. Transgenic pollen harms monarch larvae. Nature 399 20 May): p.214.

Management 22 (2) : 163-172.

Mattoo, A. and H. V. Singh, (1994), Eco-Labelling: Policy Considera-Michaels, R. G., and V. K. Smith. "Market Segmentation And Valuing Amenities With Hedonic Models: The Case Of Hazardous Waste Sites," Journal of Urban Economics, 1990 28(2), 223-242.

Nicholson-Lord, D., (1993) 'Tis the Season to be Green, The Independent, 20 December

Nuttall, N., (1993), Shoppers can cross green products off their lists, The Times, 3 July

OCDE/GD(97)105. Paris, OECD. 81p.

OECD. "Ec-labelling: Actual Effects of Selected Programmes," OCDE/GD (97) 105, 1997, Paris. (available on line at http://www.oecd.org/env/eco/books.htm#trademono)

OECD. 1997a. Case study on eco-labeling schemes. Paris, OECD (30 Dec):

OECD. 1997b. Eco-labeling: Actual Effects of Selected Programs.

Osborne, L. "Market Structure, Hedonic Models, and the Valuation of Environmental Amenities." Unpublished Ph.D. dissertation. North Carolina State University, 1995.

Osborne, L., and V. K. Smith. "Environmental Amenities, Product Differentiation, and market Power," Mimeo, 1997.

Ozanne, L.K. and Vlosky, R.P. 1996. Wood products environmental certification: the United States perspective". Forestry Chronicle 72 (2) : 157-165.

Palmquist, R. B., F. M. Roka, and T.Vukina. "Hog Operations, Environmental Effects, and Residential Property Values," Land Economics 73(1), (1997): 114-24.

Palmquist, R.B. "Hedonic Methods," in J.B Braden and C.D. Kolstad, eds. Measuring the Demand for Environmental Improvement. Amsterdam, NL: Elsevier, 1991.

Pento, T. 1997. Implementation of Public Green Procurement Programs (22-31) in Greener Purchasing: Opportunities and Innovations. Sheffield, Greenleaf Publ. 325 p.

Polak, J. and Bergholm, K. 1997. Eco-labeling and trade: a cooperative approach (Jan.): Policy in a Green Market. Environmental and Resource Economics 22, 419-

Poore, M.E.D. et al. 1989. No timber without trees. London, Earthscan. 352p.

Raff, D. M.G., and M. Trajtenberg. "Quality-Adjusted Prices for the American Automobile Industry: 1906-1940." NBER Working Paper Series, Working Paper No. 5035, February 1995.

Roberts, J. T. 1998. Emerging global environment standards: prospects and perils. Journal of Developing Societies 14 (1): 144-163.

Rosen, S., "Hedonic Prices and Implicit Markets: Product Differentiation in Pure Competition." Journal of Political Economy. 82: 34-55 (1974).

Ross, B. 1997. Eco-friendly procurement training course for UN HCR. : 126 p.

Salzman, J. 1997. Informing the Green Consumer: The Debate over the Use and Abuse of Environmental Labels. Journal of Industrial Ecology 1 (2): 11-22.

Sanders, W. 1997. Environmentally Preferable Purchasing: The US Experience (946-960) in Greener Purchasing: Opportunities and Innovations. Sheffield, Greenleaf Publ. 325p.

Sayre, D. 1996. Inside ISO 14000: The competitive advantage of environmental management. Delray Beach FL., St. Lucie Press. 232p.

SHAPIRO, C. Premiums for High Quality Products as Returns to Reputa- tion. Quarterly Journal of Economics, Vol. 98, No. 4 (1983), pp. 659-680.

Stillwell, M. and van Dyke, B. 1999. An activists handbook on genetically modified organisms and the WTO. Washington DC., The Consumer's Choice Council: 20 p.

Semenzato, A.; Costantini, A.; Meloni, M.; Maramaldi, G.; Meneghin, M.; Baratto, G. Formulating O/W Emulsions with Plant-Based Actives: A Stability Challenge for an Eective Product. Cosmetics 2018, 5, 59.

Teisl, M. F., B. Roe, and R. L. Hicks. "Can Eco-labels tune a market? Evidence from dolphin-safe labeling," Presented paper at the 1997 American Agricultural Economics Association Meetings, Toronto.

www.futureplc.com

He F C, Li Y, Yang X M, Qin F 2017 Exploration on the development path of old industrial base transition:taking Xuzhou city as an example to establish a national Eco-garden city J. Chinese Landscape Architecture. 33 91-95

Tibor, T. and Feldman, I. 1995. ISO 14000: a guide to the new environmental management standards. Burr Ridge Ill., Irwin Professional Publ. 250 p.

Du L P 2009 Some thoughts on the present situation of the application of ground cover plants J. Northern Horticulture. 08 229-231

Du H Z, Song W 1996 A brief analysis of ecological benefits of greening in Song Qingling cemetery J. Journal of Jiangsu Forestry & Technology. S1 88-91

Townsend, M. 1998. Making things greener: motivations and influences in the greening of manufacturing. Aldershot, England, Ashgate Publisher. 203p.

U.S. Energy Information Administration, What is U.S. Electricity Generation by Energy Source?, Retrieved From: https://www.eia.gov/tools/faqs/faq.php?id=427&t=3

U.S. Energy Information Administration, Biomass Explained, Retrieved From: https://www.eia.gov/energyexplained/?page=biomass_home

U.S. Environmental Protection Agency. National Water Quality Fact Inventory: 1990 Report to Congress. EPA 503-9-92-006, Apr. 1992.

UK Eco-labelling Board website, accessed via http://www.ecosite.co.uk/Ecolabel-UK/

US EPA, 1993. Determinants of effectiveness for environmental certification and labeling programs. Washington, D.C., US Environmental Protect

US EPA, 1993. Status report on the use of environmental labels worldwide. Washington, D.C., US Environmental Protection Agency (742-R-93-001 September).

US EPA, 1993. The use of life-cycle assessment in environmental labeling. Washington, D.C., US Environmental Protection Agency (742-R-93-003 September).

Wang L Y 1994 How to improve the ecological benefits in the construction of Jinan garden J. Chinese Landscape Architecture. 03 56-58+55

US EPA, 1998. Environmental labeling: issues, policies, and practices worldwide.

US EPA, 1999. Comprehensive procurement guidelines (CPG) program. Washington, D.C., US Environmental Protection Agency: <www.epa.gov/cpg>

US EPA, 1999. Environmentally preferable purchasing program: Private sector pioneers: How companies are incorporating environmentally preferable purchases. Washington, D.C.,

USG, 1993. Federal acquisition, recycling, and waste prevention. Washington DC., Executive Order: (20 October).

USG, 1998. Greening the government through waste prevention, recycling, and federal acquisition. Washington, D.C., Executive Order 13101 (September).

Kijjoa, A.; Sawangwong, P. Drugs and Cosmetics from the Sea. Mar. Drugs 2004, 2, 73–82. [CrossRef]

Wang, J.; Pan, L.; Wu, S.; Lu, L.; Xu, Y.; Zhu, Y.; Guo, M.; Zhuang, S. Recent Advances on Endocrine Disrupting Eects of UV Filters. Int. J. Environ. Res. Public Health 2016, 13, 782.

Bilal, A.I.; Tilahun, Z.; Shimels, T.; Gelan, Y.B.; Osman, E.D. Cosmetics Utilization Practice in Jigjiga Town, Eastern Ethiopia: A Community Based Cross-Sectional Study. Cosmetics 2016, 3, 40.

Ting, C.T.; Hsieh, C.M.; Chang, H.-P.; Chen, H.-S. Environmental Consciousness and Green Customer Behavior: The Moderating Roles of Incentive Mechanisms. Sustainability 2019, 11, 819.

Chen, K.; Deng, T. Research on the Green Purchase Intentions from the Perspective of Product Knowledge. Sustainability 2016, 8, 943.

Wang, H.; Ma, B.; Bai, R. How Does Green Product Knowledge Eectively Promote Green Purchase Intention? Sustainability 2019, 11, 1193.

Nguyen, T.T.H.; Yang, Z.; Nguyen, N.; Johnson, L.W.; Cao, T.K. Greenwash and Green Purchase Intention: The Mediating Role of Green Skepticism. Sustainability 2019, 11, 2653.

Cinelli, P.; Coltelli, M.B.; Signori, F.; Morganti, P.; Lazzeri, A. Cosmetic Packaging to Save the Environment: Future Perspectives. Cosmetics 2019, 6, 26.

Eixarch, H.; Wyness, L.; Siband, M. The Regulation of Personalized Cosmetics in the EU. Cosmetics 2019, 6, 29.

**CANADA SILVER BEAVER BADGE**

**Participate in our Online Classes to earn these exclusive digital badges!**
**www.toptenaward.org**

**Design & Development by:**

**Tara Asadi**

**CANADA BRONZE BEAVER BADGE**

**Participate in our Online Classes to earn these exclusive digital badges!**
**www.toptenaward.org**

**Design & Development by:**

**Tara Asadi**

**CANADA GOLD BEAVER BADGE**

**Participate in our Online Classes to earn these exclusive digital badges!**

**Design & Development by:**

**Tara Asadi**

# Environmental Lifestyle Guide

## For Grade 9

## For  Grade 10

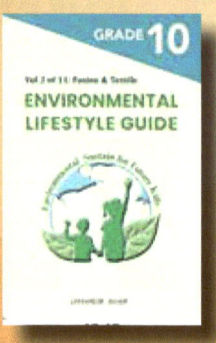
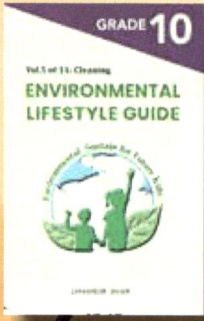
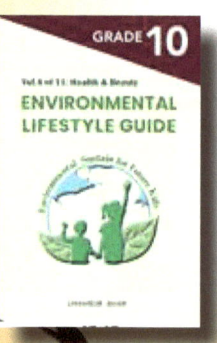

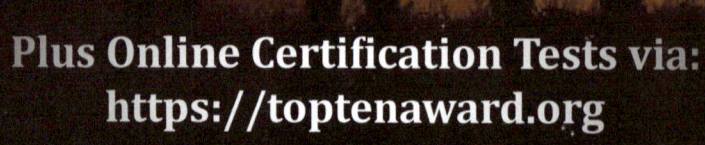

**Plus Online Certification Tests via:**
**https://toptenaward.org**

# Standard Text Books

## For Grade 11

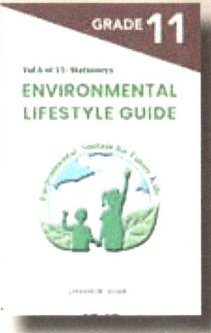  

## For Grade 12

**Environmental Lifestyle Guide**
**Standard Text Book**
For Students Grade 9 to 12
Available in more than
39,000 Bookstores
all over the globe.
https://ecofriendlyeducation.com

Cooperation by:
**Top Ten Award International Network**
**&**
**Environmental Sustain for Future Kids**

www.ingramcontent.com/pod-product-compliance
Lightning Source LLC
Chambersburg PA
CBHW040859120626
46551CB00001B/80